INTRODUCTI○

COLMAN'S CONNECTIONS

Colman's Mustard is an iconic brand known to households all over the world. It all started in Norfolk in 1814, with flour miller Jeremiah Colman.

This booklet is part of Colman's Connections, an intergenerational project which has seen Norwich residents become Colman's Detectives, researching the First World War history of this important firm.

This community research project was organised and developed by Norwich Heritage Economic and Regeneration Trust (HEART) and received funding from the Heritage Lottery Fund (HLF).

The *Colman's Connections* booklet presents an extraordinary undertaking, researched and written by the Colman's Detectives, revealing real-life stories about Colman's employees and how their lives were shaped by the conflict.

Looking back at the last 200 years, it is possible to chart the course of Colman's, from its humble beginnings at Stoke Holy Cross to the commercial powerhouse which transformed Norwich and became globally renowned. Colman's is considerably more than just a local mustard company.

By the time war was declared, Colman's had blossomed into the city's most prosperous business. The company was celebrating its centenary, and employing more workers than any other organisation

in the area. In an age characterised by child labour, unsafe working environments, long hours and low pay, the Colman family were pioneers in social welfare.

The company created health and welfare schemes, schools and nurseries, sports clubs and a canteen when such provisions were not commonplace. New homes and accommodation were built to house workers, and employees were even insured against sickness and injury. This 'from cradle to grave' protection was revolutionary, established fifty years before the creation of the welfare state.

When their workers joined the war effort, both at home and abroad, great care was taken to make their voices heard by the people of Norwich. As the city's largest employer at the time, the story of Colman's during the war years offers an invaluable insight into the lives of people in Norwich 100 years ago. It is this unique local history that the Colman's Connections project wishes to share with the city.

COLMAN'S CONNECTIONS

heritage lottery fund
LOTTERY FUNDED

Norwich HEART
HERITAGE ECONOMIC & REGENERATION TRUST

CARROW WORKS

A COMPANY MAGAZINE

WARTIME EDITIONS OF *CARROW WORKS* MAGAZINES

© Norwich HEART

Colman's produced a quarterly magazine for its workers called *Carrow Works Magazine*. This fantastic resource reveals engaging stories about the real-life experiences of Colman's workers and how their lives were affected by the First World War, and has been central to the research undertaken as a part of the Colman's Connections project.

The magazine had its origins in the late nineteenth century when Caroline Colman introduced the

Carrow Works Almanac, given to every employee at Christmas. The first edition of *Carrow Works Magazine* was published in October 1907. Costing one penny, it was published quarterly in October, January, April and July. The cover, with its Art Nouveau styling, implied a magazine of cultural worth. This was further boosted by a letter from Buckingham Palace, reproduced in the second issue, stating that Queen Alexandra was 'looking forward with much interest to perusing the first issue of the *Carrow Works Magazine*'.

The magazine had a specific ethos:

> We desire that our columns should not only prove interesting and entertaining, but that they should also tend to elevate and instruct. Further that articles dealing with Religion and Philanthropic work, Science, Art, Music, Photography, Gardening, Holiday Trips, Sports and Pastimes, and a number of kindred subjects will from time to time be inserted.

The first editor was Francis Ruben Widdows, who had joined Colman's in 1877 as a draughtsman. A member of the Institute of Mechanical Engineers, Widdows was involved with engineering classes at the Norwich Technical Institute. His views on the importance of education, coupled with the paternalistic attitude of Colman's as a company, accounts for the magazine's instructive manner.

Although Francis Widdows retired due to ill health in 1910, the gift of an invalid chair from the staff enabled him to carry on his editorial role for the magazine. Aged sixty-two at the beginning of the war, he was a product of an earlier age which may explain the tone of the magazine, especially in regards to morals, class and gender. He was not without his humour though, which is visible throughout the publication. When he finally left the magazine in 1924 he remarked, 'my health is all right but my joints are all wrong.'

LETTER FROM BUCKINGHAM PALACE

BUCKINGHAM PALACE.

28th. October 1907.

Dear Sir,

I have had the pleasure of submitting to The Queen your letter of the 11th. Instant, together with the Paper which accompanied it, and I am now commanded by Her Majesty to thank you for the same, and to add, that she is looking forward with much interest to perusing the first issue of the "Carrow Works' Magazine" which you have been so good as to send her.

I must apologise for the delay in replying to your communication, but, owing to The Queen's absence from England, I have only just had an opportunity of submitting the publication to Her Majesty.

Yours faithfully

Sidney Greville

Private Secretary.

F. R. Widdows, Esq.,

Editor

"Carrow Works' Magazine."

FRANCIS RUBEN WIDDOWS, FIRST EDITOR OF *CARROW WORKS MAGAZINE*

THE WAR YEARS

The war had an impact on the magazine's content. The October 1914 edition, the first since the outbreak, published the names and departments of those who had volunteered for service. When conscription was introduced in January 1916, *Carrow Works Magazine* stopped publishing the lists.

The names of all those killed in action were documented in the 'Roll of Honour', a sombre feature included from October 1915. This consisted of a photograph along with an obituary of those who had given the 'ultimate sacrifice'. As the war progressed, *Carrow Works Magazine* increasingly focused on the conflict, including letters from the front, with the 'Young Carrow' section and the club and society information being sacrificed.

Unlike in newspapers, the birth, marriage and death listings in the magazine were free for workers. Death notices highlight that life for those at home could also be cruelly cut short, such as the birth and death notices for Herbert Farrow in consecutive magazines, who died aged six days old. The magazine also detailed those at Carrow who joined 'Committees for the Relief of Distress occasioned by the War'. It was perhaps indicative of the class system of the time that it was mainly those of the upper classes volunteering at home who were recorded by name. However, the 'Household Hints' section of the magazine straddled the class divide, with tips on how to tell if an egg is fresh appearing alongside how to cut silk and clean ivory.

The magazine did have a lighter tone, with jokes appearing in every issue, such as in the 'Young Carrow' section:

"Describe water, Johnny," said the teacher. "Water," explained Johnny, "is a white fluid that turns black when you put your hands in it."

Colman's workers represented a large population from a variety of backgrounds across the city. The Colman's empire was not simply a place of employment; it was an enlarged community that became a source of comfort both on the home front and for the soldiers away from home. One way was through the magazines that were sent to the soldiers, as well as the provisions that they received. During the war years, the factory received vast quantities of personal letters and photographs from their employees in the Armed Forces and on the home front, some of which were published in *Carrow Works Magazine*.

ROLL OF HONOUR ILLUSTRATION FROM *CARROW WORKS MAGAZINE*

© From *Carrow Works Magazine*. Reproduced courtesy of Unilever

COLMAN'S
ON THE VERGE OF WAR

The early twentieth century saw rapid industrial, economic and social change across Europe. Before the First World War, industry in Britain was facing growing competition from countries like the United States of America and Germany. Economic growth had slowed down and there had been much industrial unrest during the years 1910 to 1913.

However, despite the situation elsewhere, Colman's was a flourishing company, its pioneering philanthropic practices attracting high quality staff and good managers.

In 1896, Russell Colman, the last of the partners, died, and Colman's became a limited company with capital of £1,350,000. By the beginning of the twentieth century, the company – which had been paternalistic, labour intensive and little mechanised – now began to adopt automation and different financial approaches. Evidence of changes came in 1913 with the appointment of Edwin Batterbee Southwell, who in the previous year had carried out negotiations for the acquisition of Farrows of Peterborough.

Southwell was appointed general manager in 1901, and in 1913 he became the first non-family member to be promoted to the Board of Directors. He was well-respected and liked by both Colman's employees and co-directors, and was a popular choice. Southwell was largely responsible for running the company during the war years. In 1915, he was elected as Lord Mayor of Norwich. He retired in 1919, but remained involved with the company, later becoming editor of the *Carrow Works Magazine*.

A CALL TO ARMS: CARROW RESPONDS TO KITCHENER'S CALL

Field Marshal Kitchener was made Secretary of State for War shortly after war was declared on 4 August 1914. On 11 August 1914 his call to arms, 'Your King and Country Need You', was published. Recruitment drives followed throughout the country, including at Carrow.

RECRUITING FOR SOLDIERS AT THE GATES OF CARROW WORKS

© From *Carrow Works Magazine*. Reproduced courtesy of Unilever

As a tide of patriotism swept the country, many employees joined the Armed Forces in response to the call to arms. Four active directors joined the services – Capt. F. Gordon D. Colman, 2nd Lieut. Jeremiah Colman, Capt. Geoffrey R. R. Colman and Capt. Frank Belville – together with those employees who had joined the Carrow Works Territorial Field Artillery when

IF I SHOULD DIE, THINK ONLY THIS OF ME; THAT THERE'S SOME CORNER OF A FOREIGN FIELD THAT IS FOREVER ENGLAND

Rupert Brooke, 'The Soldier'

it was formed in 1912, and those volunteering for Kitchener's 'New Army'.

Many of the workers joined the 8th Norfolk's (Service) Battalion, which was established in September 1914. It had the nickname 'Businessman's Battalion' due to the large number of shopkeepers and workers from the city and county which made up its number. As a company, Colman's supported the volunteers by offering them additional weekly allowances.

IN A FOREIGN FIELD

The years immediately prior to the First World War saw Colman's blighted by unemployment, particularly for young men reaching the age of eighteen and who had to be paid full adult wages. In 1911, the Colman's directors offered to arrange emigration for workers who had outgrown their current roles, and who could not be accommodated in other departments.

In the spring of that year the first party of sixteen lads accepted the offer, but three failed to obtain their parents' permission. On 1 June 1911, a party of sixteen young women left Norwich for Canada. They had received four weeks instruction in cookery and domestic work, generally given in the works kitchen. In 1912 and 1913 other parties left Carrow, some going to Australia as well as Canada.

At the start of the First World War, many of the young emigrants volunteered for the Canadian forces and subsequently returned to fight in Europe.

It was decided during the early days of the conflict that it would not be possible to repatriate all of those killed overseas. Special permission was given by the War Office for *Carrow Works Magazine* to publish photographs of the graves of Colman's employees. These images soon became a familiar and poignant feature of *Carrow Works Magazine*, reminding staff of their colleagues fighting abroad.

THE GRAVE OF COLMAN'S WORKER PRIVATE E. NICHOLS, IN FRANCE

© From *Carrow Works Magazine*.
Reproduced courtesy of Unilever

COLMAN'S ARRANGED EMIGRATION FOR SOME WORKERS, SUCH
AS THIS GROUP OF WOMEN WHO EMIGRATED TO CANADA IN 1911

© Image Courtesy of Norfolk County Council Library and Information Service

The impact of the war was almost immediately felt, and the factory had to respond to the difficulties it caused, ensuring, as far as possible, that work could continue with so many men having enlisted. Weekly meetings of managers were held so that the surplus hands from one department could be drafted to those where assistance was required. The club house and playing fields were placed at the disposal of the military and were quickly filled with khaki-clad figures, horses and heavy field guns.

The war affected every facet of people's lives, and the next four years were challenging for Colman's workers, both at home in Norwich and those overseas.

WORKERS
AT WAR

Between 1914 and 1918, a total of 921 Colman's employees joined the services, initially through volunteer recruitment drives, and later by conscription. Of these, ninety-three would not survive the war.

Colman's supported its employees who had volunteered to join up. At the onset of war, the Colman's directors had promised to re-employ all the workers who had volunteered. Whilst on active duty, they would be paid five shillings a week plus an extra one shilling per child. Furthermore the employees' pension scheme contributions would be paid by the company. By 31 March 1919, nearly £50,000 had been paid by Colman's.

By May 1915, demand from the front started to outstrip supply of volunteers. The newly appointed Director-General of Recruitment, Lord Edward Derby, encouraged men to voluntarily register their name, on the understanding that they would only be called up when absolutely necessary, with married men summoned only when there were no more single men available. Some 350,000 men volunteered under the so-called Derby Scheme, including employees from Carrow Works. However, even this was not enough to compensate for the casualties suffered on the battlefield. The scheme was abandoned in December 1915, and by January 1916, conscription for single men between eighteen and forty-one was introduced. This was extended four months later to include married men.

The following appeared in *Carrow Works Magazine* in January 1916, the month that conscription was introduced. Seemingly an article about Santa finding

his way in the blackout, it also reveals attitudes towards those who had not yet volunteered to fight:

> Let us hope he [Santa] finds the right chimneys, for a pop-gun intended for a younger brother would be hardly welcome by the bedside of a slacker, who had so far dodged the khaki.

Men who had not volunteered by December 1915, but were later conscripted, did not receive any of these benefits or guarantee of re-employment. Those who

FIVE CARROW RECRUITS

© Reproduced courtesy of Unilever. Colman's is a Unilever Trademark

A RETURN TO EMPLOYMENT FORM OF DISCHARGED SOLIDER ARTHUR JOHN FARROW

© Image Courtesy of Norfolk County Council
Library and Information Service

were conscripted after 12 December 1915 were given the option of withdrawing their pension pot or having it kept in safekeeping by Colman's. A memo to the staff dated December 1916 stated:

> The scale of benefits given by the Company to the families of soldiers on service will not be extended beyond those men who have been attested under Lord Derby's scheme.

A further note from Colman's in 1916:

> No obstacle whatsoever has been placed in any man's way to join or promise to join any branch of HM Forces [...] The decision to join is however viewed by this Company a personal matter between the individual and the State.

TRANSCRIPT TO ABOVE

Name Arthur John Farrow

Age 28 **Rank and Regiment** Private 40852 Essex

Date of discharge 08/04/1919

Medical report Right eye removed for bullet wound. Left forearm bullet wound, not able to lift heavy weights. Right forearm bullet wound – no disability. There is an added risk owing to loss of eye and he is unable to do work involving heavy lifting with left arm. Otherwise he is fit for employment.

WOMEN WORKERS AT CARROW WORKS

© From *Carrow Works Magazine*. Reproduced courtesy of Unilever

Discharged soldiers had to undergo a thorough medical examination by a Dr Fielding before being allowed to return to work. The examination was documented on pink printed forms with handwritten notes by the doctor. Many note that the employee had no wounds, no illness, and was fit for employment. Others were more telling, with incidents of shell shock, malaria, gas poisoning, trench foot, wounds, hernias and amputations. It is interesting to note that some with quite serious injuries were deemed fit to return to work.

A CHANGING WORKFORCE

Colman's kept detailed records of employee numbers, listed monthly by department, gender and age group. This Employee Register shows how much the war affected certain departments of the business. The register details that half the staff of the Mustard Mill, Starch House and Counting House, and most of the Saw Mill enlisted during the war period. The Tin Box Department was particularly affected, with sixty-one of the eighty-seven men employed joining the military.

With so many men enlisting, Colman's began employing women in traditionally male roles to cover the shortfall, with Colman's stating that 'female labour [was] only introduced in the [Tin Box] department since the war began owing to the scarcity of male workers'. Colman's had always employed women, but their roles tended to be confined to box-making or packing. In August 1914, none of the 615 female staff employed by the company worked in the office. By the war's end, fifty-seven women and girls were classed as clerical staff. Overall the number of women employed at Carrow increased during the war period by fifty percent. However, extracts from *Carrow Works Magazine*s reveal that some found it hard to adapt to these dramatic changes:

> When I commenced work at Carrow forty years ago, I never thought I should live to see a vision of crêpe-de-chine and crimples bending over a long column of pounds, shillings and pence. I should almost as soon have thought of seeing a ponderous elephant poised on an office stool.

This extract appeared in the magazine's October 1916 edition:

> DEPENDS ON HOW YOU LOOK AT IT
> "Here is an anagram describing something women should know how to use," said the puzzle giver. "It is O-T-S-V-E." "I know," said the suffragette happily. "It is VOTES.""No," growled the anti; "it is STOVE."

After the war, the men returned to their usual employment, but Colman's acknowledged the women's work with some remaining in previously male-dominated areas, whilst others returned to their traditional roles as starch and mustard packers.

EVA BARBER, FOREWOMAN OF THE BLUE DEPARTMENT

© From *Carrow Works Magazine*.
Reproduced courtesy of Unilever

Even before the war, women could hold positions of authority at Colman's. In 1904, Eva Barber was appointed forewoman of the Blue Department. She had joined the firm in 1894 and had quickly been promoted. She died from influenza in 1918 after a short illness. The manager of her department wrote that she was 'a most excellent forewoman', who 'was respected by all with whom she came in contact'. These compliments are taken from her obituary, something usually the preserve of late male employees, published in *Carrow Works Magazine* in 1919.

© From *Carrow Works Magazine*. Reproduced courtesy of Unilever.

CAPTAIN GEOFFREY COLMAN

© From *Carrow Works Magazine*. Reproduced courtesy of Unilever

As a family firm, Colman's often employed many generations from one family. An example is the Dix family, who were particularly noted for their long service. William Senior served for forty years. He was one of the first carpenters employed by Colman's and took over the running of the steam engine at Carrow Works. His son Charles followed in his footsteps, working for Colman's for sixty years. Grandson William Dix served for fifty-five years and was manager of the Mustard Mill during the period of the First World War. His name regularly appears as the referee for people requiring assistance under the Employee Trust. Great-grandson Charles W. Dix managed the Mustard Department and retired in 1943 after forty-five years' service. There were so many of the Dix family at Colman's that they had their own cricket team!

With so many families in the Colman's workforce, no employees were left untouched by the impact of the war. The Colman family also suffered from the conflict, as Captain Geoffrey Colman was seriously wounded in January 1916. Whilst building a machine-gun dugout, he was hit. The bullet damaged his lung, a blood vessel, shoulder-blade and two ribs.

CARROW
A CHANGING FACTORY

The war was a huge challenge for the factory at Carrow. Significant numbers of employees, some very senior, had enlisted, and many of the works' horses had been commandeered. In addition, there was land reduction and shortage of raw materials. All of these challenges had to be faced, alongside other obstacles such as the threat of Zeppelin airship raids and the subsequent lighting restrictions which shortened hours for production and transport.

PLOUGHING UP THE FIELDS
FOR THE WAR EFFORT

© From *Carrow Works Magazine*. Reproduced courtesy of Unilever

SHORTAGES INTENSIFY

1917 saw an increase in the sinking of merchant ships by German U-boats, and a particularly bad harvest. People were encouraged to plough up available land for growing food, and land for minor crops was strictly rationed by the Norfolk War Agriculture Committee. Acreage for growing mustard seed was reduced by sixty-eight percent in Norfolk, having a dramatic effect on production at Colman's. The company's response was to eke out their supplies, altering the proportions of white and brown seed used in manufacture. Brown seed is used to give mustard its 'bite', and white seed its stability. The result was milder mustard during the war years.

The war also proved a strain in other ways. Lack of imported goods affected the supply of materials needed to produce many Colman's products. At the outbreak of war there were good supplies of timber at Carrow, but further stock that had been purchased in Canada could not be shipped. Foreign timber was practically unobtainable and stocks became dangerously low. A new British timber plant was established at considerable cost in order to meet demand.

Steel plate used for packaging was needed for the war effort, and so cardboard was substituted for tin tops and bottoms, but this was far costlier. The penny box of starch had to be replaced by a paper bag as the demand for cardboard grew.

Used for stiffening collars and cuffs, starch was a popular Colman's product, made by extracting the starch from rice imported from Bengal and Madras. As shortages intensified, and people struggled to put food on the table, production of starch for domestic use was no longer seen as a necessity and was dramatically reduced. The Colman's starch factory at Bethnal Green in London closed.

Also problematic for Colman's was the production of Laundry Blue. One of the main ingredients, ultramarine, came mainly from Germany before the war. Supplies were obtained from Reckitt & Sons Ltd of Hull, a competitor of Colman's – evidence of the spirit of cooperation which existed between the two companies during the war.

In order to protect its considerable foreign trade in Patent Barley, Colman's arranged to temporarily manufacture it in the USA.

NORWICH IN DARKNESS: LIGHTING RESTRICTIONS

The first air raids in Britain took place in January 1915, when Zeppelins attacked King's Lynn and Great Yarmouth. Lighting restrictions and blackouts were imposed as a result, hampering production at the factory. Lighting orders were posted around the city, detailing the new restrictions.

The effect of the lighting orders on Carrow Works was dramatic. Long before the working day finished, the yard was in complete darkness, especially during winter, making movement of trucks and goods difficult.

A LIGHTING ORDER FROM SEPTEMBER 1915

LIGHTING ORDER

FOR THE

CITY OF NORWICH.

I HEREBY GIVE NOTICE that in pursuance of the powers under the Defence of the Realm Regulations, H.M. Secretary of State for the Home Department has made the following Regulations :—

1. All lights, except indoor lights not visible from outside and necessary navigation or railway lights and lights on vehicles, **shall be extinguished from half-an-hour after sunset till half-an-hour before sunrise.**

2. **The lights carried on vehicles shall not be of greater brightness than is necessary for the public safety.**

   (NOTE.—An effective way of complying with this provision is to blacken the glass of the lamps, so as to prevent the flame, &c., being visible from the front of the lamp, and blacken the lower half of the reflector. Side panels in lamps should be completely blackened.)

3. Any person who shall cause or permit any vehicle to be in any street, highway, or road to which the public have access during the period to which this Order applies, shall provide such vehicle with lamps in proper working order, and so constructed, and capable of being so attached, as when lighted to display:

   (a) A white light on each side visible to a reasonable distance to the front,

   (b) A red light visible to a reasonable distance to the rear,

   and every person driving or being in charge of any such vehicle during such period as aforesaid shall keep such lamps properly trimmed, lighted and attached :

   For the purpose of this Order the word "Vehicle" shall include any bicycle, tricycle or velocipede, and any vehicle drawn or propelled by hand.

   Provided that any bicycle, tricycle, or velocipede, and any vehicle drawn or propelled by hand, or having an over-all breadth of not exceeding three feet six inches shall be deemed to comply with the requirements of this Order if it displays, in addition to the red rear light, one white light instead of two visible to the front.

4. Street lamps provided by the Local Authority may be lit in such numbers, at such points, and of such degree of brightness as may be approved of by a Competent Military Authority.

This Order is substituted for the Lighting Order dated 5th March, 1915.

(Signed) E. F. WINCH,
CHIEF CONSTABLE.

Guildhall, Norwich,
September 27th, 1915.

GIBBS & WALLER, LTD. LITHOGRAPHERS AND ACCOUNT BOOK MANUFACTURERS, COLEGATE STREET, NORWICH.

In April 1915, the *Carrow Works Magazine* reported that:

> a commercial gentleman informed us that when making the journey from Trowse Station to Thorpe after sundown in February 1915, he wondered what became of the Carrow Works. The place, usually a blaze of light, was in complete darkness. He assured us that it was only his familiarity with its exact location that enabled him to tell when he was passing Carrow.

In response to the lighting restrictions, revised working hours were introduced. From October 1916 to February 1917, the working hours for men were set at 6.45am to 5.10pm with an hour lunch, Monday to Friday, and 6.45am to 11.40am Saturdays, making a fifty-two-hour week. A special corps of Night Watchers was formed to meet any emergency that might arise from Zeppelin attacks. The company also relied on local police, the fire brigade and the Special Reserve.

COLMAN'S HORSE BOOK – HOW HORSES WERE UTILISED

HORSES.

For Trucking............................	10 horses
Spare ditto.............................	1 horse
Covered cart for City work.............	1 horse
Covered cart in the Works (Green).......	1 horse
Covered cart in the Works (Parish)......	1 horse
Carpenters cart........................	1 horse
Bricklayers carts......................	2 horses
Tumbrils for Seed and General Work......	5 horses
Light cart for General work............	1 horse
Light cart for Mustard Mill............	1 horse
Lame Horses One with Cankered Foot) One with Pricked Foot) One stopped by Police)...	3 horses
For Light work at the Stables...........	1 horse
	28
Tired Horses One for Trucking) Three for Tumbril Work)...	4 horses

Two new horses purchased this week, one of which is included in the 28 above.

WAR HORSES

In the early twentieth century, horsepower was the main method of hauling goods around Carrow Works. In 1908, there were thirty-eight horses, mostly Suffolk Punches or Norfolk Shires. Thirty-four of these were reserved for general use, whilst two were used by the fire brigade and one was kept by each of the Mustard and Building Departments.

Animal welfare was a priority at Carrow, and all horses had to be well fed and groomed and their harnesses removed during the lunch break. They spent summer evenings in the meadows around the works and weekends at Whitlingham.

THE CARROW LOCOMOTIVE ALPHA

© From Carrow Works Magazine. Reproduced courtesy of Unilever

A COLMAN'S HORSE MOVING GOODS

© From Carrow Works Magazine. Reproduced courtesy of Unilever

Colman's kept records of all horses purchased, listing the seller, price paid, history, any illnesses, and in what capacity the horses were used.

The names of the horses appear to reflect events in the country at the time. Just before the outbreak of war, names included Christabel (after the suffragette Christabel Pankhurst) and Lloyd George. The war years saw the patriotic naming of the horses after military men and battles, such as Joffre, Kitchener, Verdun and Baghdad.

In 1914 there was a massive shortfall of horses which were required for the military, and a National Emergency Impressment Order was made whereby local purchasing officers were empowered to seize horses and equipment. Records show seven horses taken by the military and the compensation paid to Colman's. A further four horses were conscripted by the military in May 1917, but were returned as they were not required. This is unusual as very few horses were returned to their original owners after the war.

Not all of the horses were so keen to join up. The *Carrow Works Magazine* of April 1915 carried a story of two of the Colman's horses, commandeered by the Army in 1914, who escaped whilst being loaded onto wagons. They galloped back to Carrow but they were collected the following morning!

Transport via rail was also difficult, due to requisition by the military, and so the company purchased its own locomotive named Alpha. This had been considered but resisted before the war. Alpha was bought from the M&GN Railway Co. at Melton Constable. The engine was already thirty-nine years old and weighed just over ten tons. However, before coming to Carrow it had been given a new interior and could easily haul ten to twelve trucks.

Twenty carters (cart drivers) were employed at Colman's in 1914, but this had dwindled to thirteen by the end of the war. By 1924, carters at Colman's ceased to be employed, demonstrating that horses had been replaced by mechanisation.

LIFE
ON THE HOME FRONT

Life at home changed dramatically during the war years. Previous conflicts, such as the Boer War, had not really impacted upon the everyday lives of British people. However, the First World War changed this, as the war was felt deeply at home in Norwich as well as on the front.

There was the very real threat of bombardment on home soil which, together with shortages of food and the mobilisation of industry for the war effort, affected all. The men who joined up were not from a regular army, and they left behind occupations that still needed to be fulfilled. Many women for the first time worked outside of the home in roles that had previously been the domain of men.

FAMILY LIFE OF THE HOME FRONT

The loss of so many young men had a profound impact on the tight-knit communities who lived around Carrow and worked at the factory. In Trowse many of the village's residents worked at Colman's, which often employed many generations of the same family.

In Trowse the names of the fallen are recorded on the village war memorial. The names of workers such as Percy Fox, Joseph Guymer, Joseph Hill, Arthur Lovick, Ernest Nichols, Charles Simmons and Percy Sword are inscribed on the memorial, and also appear on the Roll of Honour memorial at Carrow House.

The experiences of the Fox family of 11 School Terrace illustrates how deeply the war affected a family, a community and a workplace. By 1917, William Fox had worked in the Carrow gardens for over twenty years, and had five sons. Tragically two of his sons were killed in France, their names appearing on the war memorial. A third son was discharged from the Army after being gravely wounded and a fourth son was serving in India. The fifth was at that time still employed in the Mustard Mill.

THE TROWSE WAR MEMORIAL

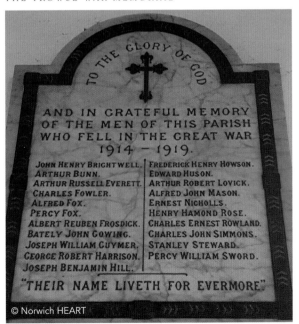

© Norwich HEART

TEA AND CHRISTMAS TREE
ENTERTAINMENT AT CARROW SCHOOL

© From *Carrow Works Magazine*. Reproduced courtesy of Unilever

GEOFFREY BARRETT'S NOTEBOOK, 1916

cannon   grenade   hospital
artillary   anti-aircraft   chloroform
lieutenant uniform   exhaustion
squadron   battalion   splinters
regiment   aerodrome   operation
sword   convoy   boracic lotion
cartridge section   medicine

© Norfolk Record Office

Children were particularly affected, as their home life became disrupted through absent parents and the deaths of family and friends. In school, children learned about the battles that were being fought and the new technology used at the front. Geoffrey Barrett, aged 10 in 1916, was a pupil at Carrow School. His exercise book is held at the Norfolk Record Office and gives a valuable insight into children's education 100 years ago. The words regiment, squadron, hospital and exhaustion appear in his spelling test, revealing how the war influenced even the most commonplace activities.

Early in the war efforts were made to provide comfort and normality to those children whose fathers had joined up. At Christmas in 1914, Mrs Colman invited the workers' families to a 'Tea and Christmas Tree Entertainment' in the Carrow Schoolrooms. After entertainment and magic tricks provided by Professor Greenie, all the children went home with a present, the mothers receiving an illustrated War Calendar.

However, by 1915 the war had become firmly enmeshed in everyday life:

One wonders how darkness will affect Christmas. Children who are on good terms with 'Santa Claus' will have to warn him to obscure his headlights and to exhibit a red rear light. He must beware anti-aircraft guns, and be prepared to show his driving licence to any zealous 'Special' who desires to see it. On no account must he use a flash-lamp or strike a match.

THE WOMAN WHO WASTES A CRUST WASTES A CARTRIDGE!

Propaganda slogan from the *Win-The-War Cookery* Book

THE KITCHEN FRONT

As war progressed, food shortages and rationing became a part of everyday life. By 1917, things had become very tough for people at home. Before the war, three fifths of all food consumed was imported from overseas, and this was becoming increasingly difficult. Not only were merchant ships being threatened by U-boats, but many were being used to transport men, food and munitions to the front. The problem was exacerbated by the fact that home-grown food was in short supply as many of the men who farmed it had gone to fight in the war.

The *Win-The-War Cookery Book* was published for the Food Economy Campaign in 1917, to show how to avoid waste in buying, cooking and eating food, particularly importantly how to save wheat, bread and flour. 'Economy for rich and poor alike' was viewed very differently. It was felt that bread was 'the chief food of the manual worker so therefore they must have it'.

Further suggestions included eating asparagus, not potatoes, and to buy the most expensive meat they could afford, leaving the cheaper cuts to the poor. Oysters, lobsters, salmon, sole and turbot were to be the choice of the wealthy in order to conserve the cheaper fish for those with less money to spend.

Carrow Works Magazine did its part in encouraging the workers to be thrifty and to cut waste. Women were urged to use any available ground, including window boxes, to cultivate herbs and vegetables, and wartime recipes were shared. New fashions were frowned upon, and women were encouraged to wear the same coat and skirt instead of purchasing new items. Men were asked to do their part by spending less on tobacco and cigarettes. A hay-box was recommended for the slow cooking of rice, vegetables and puddings. It used hay or straw to insulate boiling food and complete the cooking process, offering a real saving of gas. Recipes included:

Potted Meat Substitute
2 ozs. Haricot or butter beans, soaked overnight. Boil till tender (save water for stock). Stir in 2 ozs. grated cheese. Season and add ½ oz. margarine and a little of Colman's mustard. Heat and mix well. Put into potted meat jars and run over melted margarine to cover.

H. Jones, the Head Gardener at Carrow Gardens, offered advice on what to grow when and where. The editor of *Carrow Works Magazine* encouraged readers to go 'in for a dig, and a good, serviceable one at that', stating that it was not below one's dignity to do so, and adding that 'every patriotic individual, from Princess Mary, who tills her little plot at Windsor, downward' should be involved. The editor continued: 'delve on my patriots! In due course you shall reap your reward, and when the time comes for you to 'lift' your fine tubers, I shall be happy to furnish you with my private address.'

'Household Hints' had been a popular feature of *Carrow Works Magazine* long before the outbreak of the First World War. Much of the advice was on how to run a more efficient household, such as how to care for your clothes, furniture and kitchen utensils to make them last longer. Suggestions on how to improve the taste of food and drink included such diverse examples as making mashed potatoes 'light and creamy', 'how to make tea for invalids' and 'adding grains of salt to coffee to improve the flavour'. As the war progressed, and food and other resources were increasingly in short supply, the emphasis became much more about how to economise and make do. The tip of putting a slice of bread in the cake tin and renewing it every third day to prevent the cakes from becoming stale was in total contrast to the later war years. The price and availability of coal in the war years were a burden on many households, so the following advice was offered:

> It is important that with the present high price of coal, great economy should be exercised in the use of fuel. Unless flues, stoves, utensils etc. are kept free from soot, much heat is wasted. When the oven is heated, it should be utilised to its fullest extent, and after it has been used for baking bread, cakes, pies, etc., a few cinders slightly moistened will give enough heat for cooking stews, milk, puddings etc.

As ever there was humour in the magazine, to reflect what was going on at the time.

> Food Shortages!
> Mrs Newlywed: "Oh Hubert, I feel so ashamed! Uncle Hiram has sent us a dozen eggs and a bushel of potatoes for Christmas, and all we sent him was a diamond tie pin".

The *Win-The-War Cookery Book*, and to some extent, 'Household Hints' in *Carrow Works Magazine*, encouraged the women of Britain to consider themselves as fighting the war in their larders, in their kitchens and in their dining rooms.

FIRST WORLD WAR FASHION

Before the First World War, high fashion was a sign of wealth and a lot of effort and expense went into the many layers and accessories. Clothing was impractical with restrictive corsets, hobble skirts and large cumbersome hats.

For example, in 1915 'war crinolines' became the latest mode with their wide, full skirts deliberately flaunting yards of fabric despite its limited availability. A government initiative to implement a standard dress for women came to nothing.

During the First World War, romantic high waists and extravagant sleeves were the order of the day along with black and white magpie fashions and plenty of spots, stripes, sashes and lace. Colours were generally muted, including subdued navy blues, beiges, greys, browns and black. Khaki also made an appearance and military tailoring with embellishments such as epaulets, buttons, braids, buckles and pockets was very popular. Wool was seen as a luxury, but Coco Chanel's innovative knitted jersey made knitwear garments highly desirable. Where they could, women allowed their evening wear to be more frivolous and impractical, made from spun silk and gossamer and with shorter, more daring skirts. Whilst the Colman family would have been able to indulge in high fashion if they wished to, the majority of the population, such as those employed by Colman's, could not afford such luxuries.

1914 FASHIONS AT A COLMAN'S GARDEN PARTY

© From *Carrow Works Magazine*. Reproduced courtesy of Unilever

Colman's female employees were treated very well and would have aspired to dress nicely, but throwaway fashion was not a luxury they could afford. They may have wandered through Chamberlin's Department Store and gazed upon the latest fashions, but they were more likely to be seen in a respectable wool suit and white blouse or a cotton dress – not forgetting of course, the ubiquitous corset.

Shop girls, bank clerks and Colman's girls would still have had to think carefully about any new clothing purchase and would have resorted to buying second-hand items or making fashionable alterations and additions to their existing clothes. Colman's girls had long been able to take advantage of the sewing and cutting out classes set up initially by Caroline Colman, and held four times a week during their dinner hour. Here they were able to purchase fabric at cost price and were taught how to assemble garments. The *Carrow Works Magazine* also ran regular prize competitions which included dressmaking, knitting and laundry tasks.

WOMEN IN THEIR FINERY COLLECTING AT THE CARROW WORKS GATES

© From *Carrow Works Magazine.* Reproduced courtesy of Unilever

The war did make a difference, despite the ninety percent rise in the annual cost of women's clothing between 1914 and 1918. Many women were earning their own wages and for the first time were able to spend more on clothes and accessories. Firms such as Chamberlin's developed mass-production methods when their factories were requisitioned for the production of clothing for the Admiralty and the War Office. This led to cheaper, ready-made clothes becoming available and made fashion more accessible to the masses.

THE COLMAN'S COMMUNITY

FROM CRADLE TO GRAVE

Influenced by their strong Christian values, the Colman family are remembered for their pioneering achievements in social welfare. Colman's set up a system of nurseries, schools, medical care, housing and pensions for their workers, supporting them 'from cradle to grave'.

With a workforce of around 3,000 people, Carrow was a community in itself. Workers were able to enjoy a thriving programme of social and sporting activities supported by the company. In the years leading up to war, the *Carrow Works Magazine* carried regular information on the Social Scheme, a formal programme covering every day of the week throughout the year. Most of the activities were based at the Carrow Club House and grounds.

Sundays were primarily for meetings of the Men's and Women's First Day Schools and the Children's Sunday School. Weekday sessions for men and boys included billiards, skittles, draughts, football, physical culture and gymnastics. There were also violin and cello classes, as well as sessions for junior and senior bands and an orchestra. For women and girls, there were classes in cookery, sewing, dancing and gymnastics. The Club House Library and Reading Rooms were open every day with books available from the Lending Department. Regular concerts, lectures and dramatic performances were held, often featuring the talents of the employees themselves.

Colman's had its own Carrow Football Club team, as well as individual teams for some of the factory's departments. There were two cricket teams, the Carrow Cricket Club, and the second called 'Sinapis' (after the genus of the mustard plant) who were all Cannon Street staff and played at Nork Park, London. In addition, Carrow had draughts and rifles teams, and a swimming club. Alongside the involvement of the many sports clubs in local leagues, a number of inter-departmental competitions were held annually. Competition was particularly keen between the Mustard and Starch Departments.

CARROW FOOTBALL CLUB 1915, WINNERS OF THE NORFOLK COUNTY FOOTBALL SHIELD AND THE LOWESTOFT HOSPITAL CUP

© From *Carrow Works Magazine*. Reproduced courtesy of Unilever

CARROW CLUB HOUSE IN MILITARY OCCUPATION

© Image Courtesy of Norfolk County Council Library and Information Service

When war broke out, all sporting and social activities were affected as the Club House and playing fields were placed at the disposal of the military authorities. Carrow and Sinapis Cricket Clubs both ended their seasons prematurely, although Carrow Football Club carried on playing some friendly matches against military units stationed in the area. Carrow Ladies Hockey Team also maintained a programme of fixtures. In the Club House, regular concerts for soldiers were organised by the Misses Colman and Mrs Stuart, with many others connected with Carrow giving their services.

CARROW SUNDAY SCHOOL

The Carrow Sunday School had started in 1840 when Colman's was still based at Stoke Holy Cross. By the time of its 75th anniversary in 1915, there were 420 pupils on the books with an average attendance of just over 300. The children were treated to an annual summer outing – a river trip to Whitlingham or a railway excursion to Cromer. However, during the war, these days out were stopped due to the disruption of the railway system. It was decided instead to hold the children's annual treat at the Club House grounds, with afternoon tea included. The saving in costs of £10 was sent to the Norwich War Hospital Supply Depot.

SUNDAY SCHOOL SLOW BICYCLE RACE

© From *Carrow Works Magazine*. Reproduced courtesy of Unilever

Events included running fifty yards, then threading a needle and running back to the start; a sash race, where girls pulled flags from a pole then ran with their waists encircled by the sashes, and a slow bicycle race, where the winner comes in last.

AN INDUSTRIAL COMMUNITY

The mid to late nineteenth century witnessed the establishment of 'model villages' by such philanthropic industrialists as the Lever Brothers at Port Sunlight and Cadbury's at Bourneville. The village of Trowse, on the outskirts of Norwich and close to Carrow, is an example of this style of industrial community.

Colman's financial records evidence the large amount of land bought up by the family around their factory at Carrow. Due to the collapse of the textile industry, land and labour were cheap and plentiful in Norwich. Statistics show that by 1893, over 2,000 inhabitants of the city were Colman's employees, the majority of the workforce living within the vicinity of Carrow.

The Colmans were responsible for the transformation of Trowse to the one that we recognise today. The first cottages were built with distinctive red brick and originally had mustard-coloured front doors. As part of Colman's paternalistic and educational ethos, the seventeenth-century Manor House was restored and extended as a reading room in around 1899. Also built was a Congregational Chapel, now demolished, but a place of worship for Colman's casualties of war. Where Colman's differed from their temperance-minded benevolent counterparts, however, was that the residents at Trowse were allowed not just one pub, but two.

The 1911 census reveals just how reliant the village of Trowse was on Colman's for employment, with many recording the 'mustard works' as their place of work. The terraced houses consisted of five or six rooms with as many as ten people to a house. Some even took in lodgers to help make ends meet. Infant mortality was high. School Terrace, consisting of only eighteen houses, had an infant mortality rate of twenty one percent.

Many of the workers from Trowse joined up to fight. Joseph Guymer, a member of the Trowse Congregational Church, was awarded the Military Medal for conspicuous bravery on the Western Front, having carried important messages under heavy shell fire. After morning service on one of his visits home, Joseph was presented with a silver watch as a memento by Mr Colman himself.

On 28 May 1919, the parishioners of Trowse gave a welcome home dinner and social event to forty-four soldiers who returned from the conflict. The event was presided over by Mr R. J. Colman, along with Mrs Colman and Captain and Mrs Geoffrey Colman, further demonstrating the links between the Colman's and Trowse.

CARROW SCHOOL

Decades before education became compulsory for children in England, Colman's set up schools for their employees' children. Carrow School was established in 1857 by Jeremiah James Colman, setting out his philosophy in a letter to his workforce:

> In these days of progress, that man is sure to be left far behind, who has neglected the cultivation of his intellect while he who strives to improve his mind stands a fair chance of raising himself in the social scale.

The school was so successful that new buildings, designed especially for the purpose on Carrow Hill, were built, with the entire cost being funded by the company. The school's fees, initially of one penny per week, were used to provide prizes at the Christmas and Midsummer prize-giving.

In addition to subjects required by the Education Code, attention was paid to practical skills. Boys were taught drawing, modeling in clay, Venetian ironwork, gardening and beekeeping. The girls had lessons in cookery, needlework, basketwork and domestic economy.

Having been a pupil, pupil-teacher and assistant master, John Olorenshaw was appointed Headmaster in 1899. He is an example of the loyalty and continuity

CARROW SCHOOL

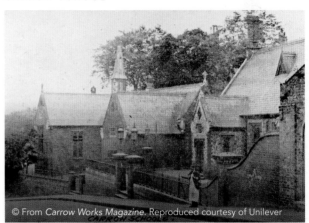

© From *Carrow Works Magazine*. Reproduced courtesy of Unilever

of service that the Colman family inspired, serving as Headmaster throughout the war years, finally retiring in 1925.

By 1914, the school on Carrow Hill had become too small, and there were plans to relocate it to new premises on City Road. The building, named Lakenham Council School, was completed in the summer, but with the outbreak of war the premises were requisitioned and used as a military hospital. It was not until five years later that Carrow School was finally closed in November 1919, and the pupils transferred to the new school, with John Olorenshaw in post as Headmaster. The official opening ceremony took place on Armistice Day with members of the Colman family present.

THE CARROW WORKS' KITCHEN

In 1868, the first Carrow Works' Kitchen was started by Caroline Colman in a small lean-to building in the old stable yard. Her aim was to provide the workers with coffee, hot meat and potatoes with gravy at cost price,

AT WORK IN THE KITCHEN, 1910/11

© From *Carrow Works Magazine*. Reproduced courtesy of Unilever

the firm covering the cooking expenses. By 1911, the kitchen was 'replete with all requisite appliances for successful cookery' and embraced a very large and varied menu.

The war years were challenging for those who worked and supervised the kitchen. The Social Scheme Committee had sympathy for the 'many difficulties which surround all catering under the present abnormal conditions', whilst the magazine editor commented:

> ...one never knows what is to be obtained in the shape of food, this leads one to feel very sympathetic towards Caterers and Housekeepers. Their capabilities are being most severely taxed by now, and it would seem almost a crime to complain about anything that may be put on the table.

The *Carrow Works Magazine* provided annual reports by the lady superintendent of the kitchen, giving us a partial insight into the kinds of food and drink provided and the wider conditions at the factory.

In 1914, there was an initial decline in the amount of food and drink served at the kitchen, as many workers volunteered to fight. By 1915, the composition of the workforce at Colman's had changed. There was a large increase in the number of girls, and the provision of food and drinks increased accordingly, with the exception of cocoa and fruit drinks.

In 1917, there was a reduction in refreshments supplied, reflecting the change to the 'Eight Hour Day' adopted at Carrow Works, and the kitchen did not open until 8.25am. By 1918, the workforce had dropped significantly, the canteen was running reduced hours, and there were shortages in a number of foods, such as imports of tea and coffee.

The later war years certainly saw a marked fall in the number of dinners and drinks. Although we cannot determine what food was served, it is clear that Colman's continued to support their staff through this period with cheap access to food and drink whilst at work.

CLUBS, CARE AND COFFINS

The Colman family encouraged their workers to 'help themselves' through clubs dedicated to good works, thrift and money saving. Inspired by the Friends' First Day School in Norwich, run by Quakers, the Colman's set up similar schools at Carrow. The Carrow First Day Schools not only administered non-denominational religious instruction, but instigated a Savings Bank, Clothing Club, Sick Club and Coal Club. It also ran a Self-help Society, established for the moral and material benefit of the members. In 1907,

average attendance exceeded 200 men and over 100 women, meeting on Sunday mornings and afternoons respectively.

The Savings Club, opened in 1899, offered an interest rate of 4% on savings to members. By 1914, it had 164 members. Interestingly, given the pressures of war and rationing, by 1918 the membership had increased to 185. The Clothing Club showed a similar determination by Colman's employees to carry on as usual during the First World War, with the 1914 records showing 2,000 depositors.

The Pension Scheme was introduced in 1899 as a memorial to Jeremiah James Colman. A minimum of two pence per week was deducted from members' pay, with a commitment the company would provide a pension of eight shillings a week for men reaching the age of sixty-five. Membership of the scheme during the First World War decreased. Although there were many women and temporary staff working at Colman's over this period, they were ineligible to join.

Colman's Employees' Trust was established in 1898 under the terms of Jeremiah James Colman's will, which left £2,000 annually for a period of twenty years. By 1918, the Trustees had considered over 6,000 applications for assistance including nursing and food for the sick, the supply of appliances, and the provision of warm and suitable clothing for children. In addition, Colman's offered grants to employees absent due to disease, and, to accelerate recovery after illness, sent over 1,000 people to convalescent homes or for breaks at the seaside.

COMPANY MEMO DETAILING THE TYPES OF COFFINS
PROVIDED, DEPENDING ON POSITION

COMPANY MEMO DETAILING THE TYPES OF COFFINS
PROVIDED, DEPENDING ON POSITION

COPY.

18th May 1906.

FUNERALS.

Carrow Works Rules as to allowances by J. & J.C.Ltd.
for Funerals of Employees and their relatives.

Note:- Pensioners are considered as Employees.

Staff. Shell and polished oak coffin, with brass furniture, brass plate, trimmings and linings, will be supplied, and workmen's time as bearers paid for, if required by relatives.
For wives and children of members of Staff, a polished oak coffin and brass plate will be supplied.

Foremen. For Foremen, their wives or children, a plain oak coffin, with brass plate, will be supplied.

Employees. other than above. For men or women, boys or girls, and the wives and children of men employed, and dependent upon them, a red deal coffin, with ordinary lettered plates, will be supplied.
If request be made for an oak coffin, it will be supplied but a charge of 10/- will be made in the case of an adult to cover extra cost.
In the case of oak coffins being required for children, a less charge than 10/- will be made according to circumstances.

Bearers

The Employees' Trust helped seventy people with the cost of operations. Fifty-seven people were sent for treatment at the spa towns of Bath, Buxton and Harrogate, and thirteen patients were sent to Kelling Sanatorium, epileptic homes or asylums. 517 people went to convalescent homes around England and a further 737 people were helped to recuperate through breaks at the seaside or in the country. The 'necessities' included 205 elastic stockings, 226 spectacles, 208 trusses, and other appliances, including artificial eyes!

By 1918, the legacy had been fulfilled and the remaining balance only used for pensioners or medical equipment. A letter dated 19 October 1918 sets out the company's policy: 'only the first truss would be supplied free, [they] would not provide elastic stockings for varicose veins and half wages would be paid in the event of scarlet fever or diphtheria'!

Finally, the Colman's support extended to families' needs at the end of their lives when there was provision for coffins and shrouds. All coffins made were recorded in the 'Coffin Book', now held at Unilever Archives, which detailed the date, name, address and department of the deceased. The style of coffin, type of wood used, and fixtures and fittings depended on the worker's rank within the company. Each coffin was made to measure and worked on by two carpenters and an apprentice.

Half a day was allowed to attend the funeral of 'a wife, husband, child, father, mother, brother, sister', and workers were permitted to take off a maximum of one day to make funeral arrangements.

© From *Carrow Works Magazine*. Reproduced courtesy of Unilever

PENSIONERS AT THE DELL

Colman's were pioneers in employee healthcare, providing homes for their pensioners at The Dell in Trowse. *A Souvenir of a Visit to Carrow Works* published in 1908 describes in idyllic terms the two dozen almshouses provided. Positioned in a natural dell sheltered by high trees, the cottages form three sides of a square, with a lawn and neat gardens in the centre. The occupants were married couples or widows of retired employees, as well as a trained nurse. The residents of The Dell did their share for the war effort too, making shirts and undergarments for soldiers, for which they provided the material themselves.

Residents Mr and Mrs Beckwith celebrated their golden wedding on 27 October 1917. Mr Beckwith had retired in June 1911, after working for Colman's for forty-one years. Like many other pensioners, Mr Beckwith volunteered to return to work at the factory shortly after the outbreak of war. However, any pensioners who re-joined Colman's as temporary workers during the war had their pensions suspended.

At the onset of war, The Dell's resident nurse was a German-born woman. She was leaving Norwich for another job, but wanted to be able to return, and the police requested a bond from Colman's so that she could do so. At that time foreigners were regarded with suspicion, with the threat of spying a particular fear. Concerns regarding the nurse were discussed at a board meeting on 6 November 1916. There was no explanation as to why it was so 'undesirable' for her to return to the area, as she had been in the service of Colman's for thirty years. Whatever the reason, Colman's did not issue a bond for her good behaviour and she left Norwich, although the company did provide her with an annuity.

DO YOUR BIT

THE WAR EFFORT AT HOME

During the war everyone was expected to 'do their bit' to help the war effort. Whether through fundraising, donating items or volunteering time, the Colman's staff and family looked for ways of supporting the war from the home front.

FUNDRAISING FOR THE WAR EFFORT

From the start of the war in August 1914 to the Armistice in 1918, Colman's workers and their families demonstrated unceasing generosity in their support for organisations associated with the war effort. This was shown through a range of events and activities, all the more impressive as these families were not the most affluent in the city.

Contributions from Carrow workers towards the costs of soldiers' hospital beds were collected through the Hospital Saturday and Sunday Fund and totalled around £200 a year. In a letter of thanks dated 20 December 1916, the Chairman of the Board of Management at the Norfolk and Norwich Hospital told contributors that:

> as the result of their help, about one hundred beds, out of a total of two-hundred and fifty-four for military patients, have been maintained during the past year without encroaching upon the general income of the Hospital.

Carrow workers also maintained a constant supply of food and 'comforts' for recovering soldiers with several departments organising weekly collections. The girls of the Starch Packing and Paper Box Departments decided that something non-perishable ought to accompany food items, and a gramophone was dispatched to Lakenham Military Hospital together with a supply of records.

GRAMOPHONE PRESENTED BY THE GIRLS OF THE STARCH PACKING AND PAPER BOX DEPARTMENTS TO LAKENHAM MILITARY HOSPITAL

© From *Carrow Works Magazine*. Reproduced courtesy of Unilever

'OUR DAY' COLLECTION AT CARROW
WORKS GATE, SATURDAY 28 OCTOBER 1916

PERFORMANCE OF *BLUE BEARD AND FATIMA*
AT THE CLUB HOUSE

© From Carrow Works Magazine. Reproduced courtesy of Unilever

© From *Carrow Works Magazine*. Reproduced courtesy of Unilever

Throughout the war years various events were organised on Colman's premises to help war charities. Concerts were organised at the Club House and in January 1915 a performance by the Carrow Girls' Gymnastic and Singing Classes included *Blue Beard and Fatima,* with the proceeds going to the Red Cross Society.

A fete in Carrow Gardens in June 1917 raised over £800 and attracted around 6,000 people. Occasionally, there were street collections at Carrow gates.

Alexandra Day in October 1914 was marked with a sale of pink wild roses, manufactured by the inmates of the John Groom Crippleage Mission. These collections were a comparatively new institution but were also taken up by the Norfolk Branch of the Red Cross Society under the title of 'Our Day'. Initially, Morse, the nursery firm, gave 23,000 roses for sale in Norwich, but in later years white flags bearing the Red Cross of Geneva were distributed.

Not to be outdone by the adults, the Sunday School children did their bit to fundraise too. Although the Sunday School held a gift service annually for those in sickness or in need across Norwich, the war saw a change to those who benefitted.

CARROW WORKERS AT NORWICH TANK WEEK

© From *Carrow Works Magazine*. Reproduced courtesy of Unilever

Throughout the war the Sunday School children were encouraged to support the war effort for those both at home as well as abroad. An egg collection held in April 1918 saw 400 eggs accumulated for future winter use and for the wounded soldiers in the hospitals of the district.

Miss Mary M. Montgomerie acknowledged a gift for the Bracondale Voluntary Aid Detachment Hospital:

> Thank you so very much for the beautiful supply of eggs received here. Please tell the Carrow Schools children how grateful we are for them.

Norwich Tank Week, organised by the Norwich Branch of the National Union of Women Workers, was held from 1 to 6 April 1918 in Norwich market place. The ladies of Carrow played their part in this fundraising event, and girls from each of the leading departments attended, with the permission of the directors. An amount of £1,288 4sh 0d was raised by the women and girls of Carrow Works, along with some private contributions.

In December 1914, it was decided to donate gifts to those Belgian refugees who had come to England after the German invasion. Items of clothes and toys

CARROW (BRACONDALE WOODS) AUXILIARY RED
CROSS HOSPITAL – PATIENTS AND STAFF

© From *Carrow Works Magazine*. Reproduced courtesy of Unilever

were given along with money to buy boots. Between
August 1914 and May 1915, some 250,000 Belgians
fled to England. Some of these were offered shelter in
the Norfolk area and collections were held for these
refugees at Carrow Works.

Overheard on Flag Day
Collector: "Will you not help the Belgians?"
Old Lady: "Why, my dear, I am helping them. I've
just ordered some Brussels sprouts."

In December 1915, it was decided that gifts should
be for those in the war zones of France and Flanders:
'it was expected that the gifts understandably would
be less than previous years however many more items
were sent.'

WOUNDED SOLDIERS AND MILITARY HOSPITALS

Wounded soldiers became a common feature of life
in Norwich, and Colman's workers were quick to offer
their support, many volunteering with the Red Cross
or helping at local hospitals. Serious casualties were
treated at the three military hospitals: the Norfolk
and Norwich Hospital, the Norfolk War Hospital
(Thorpe St. Andrew), and the Lakenham Military
Hospital (occupying the Council School). These were
supplemented by a network of Auxiliary Red Cross
Military Hospitals in village halls, public buildings, and
large private residences.

Colman's offered premises at Bracondale Woods for
an Auxiliary Military Hospital, where the County Hall
car park now stands. With accommodation for thirty-

CERTIFICATE SHOWING A COLLECTION FROM CARROW SUNDAY SCHOOL FOR THE SERBIAN RELIEF FUND

CARROW WORKS CONTINGENT OF THE NORFOLK BRANCH (NORWICH DIVISION) MEN'S DETACHMENTS OF THE BRITISH RED CROSS SOCIETY

© From *Carrow Works Magazine*. Reproduced courtesy of Unilever

© From *Carrow Works Magazine*. Reproduced courtesy of Unilever

two patients, the hospital had eight well-appointed wards, a surgery fitted with an electric bath and 'necessary appliances', a billiard room, and a dining room which was also used as a recreation room. The Matron was a Miss Hamilton, and the Sister was a Miss M. A. Hopper. Patients were encouraged to take up home skills and concert parties were laid on. On Sundays, services were held by a clergyman of the Anglican Church and a Nonconformist minister. The hospital eventually closed on 15 February 1919 having admitted 340 patients, and Miss Hopper was later awarded the medal of the Royal Red Cross (2nd Class).

Regular supplies were sent to the hospitals by the workforce, and the members of the Carrow First Day School visited the local military hospitals 'in order to minister creature comforts and encouragement to

those who have risked life and limb in the service of their King and Country'.

Many employees volunteered to help wounded soldiers returning from the front. The Voluntary Aid Detachments (VADs) were established with the help of the Red Cross and Order of St. John to provide field nursing services, mainly in hospitals, in the United Kingdom and other countries in the British Empire.

Workers at Colman's were quick to come forward when war was declared, many of them joining local VADs or offering themselves for other support roles. Blanche Bush and Maude Lovick from the Starch Packing Floor at Carrow Works volunteered to help VAD members at Bracondale Red Cross Hospital on Saturday and Sunday afternoons and evenings. Blanche Bush began

VAD MEMBER
BLANCHE BUSH

VAD MEMBER
MAUDE LOVICK

© From *Carrow Works Magazine*.
Reproduced courtesy of Unilever

© From *Carrow Works Magazine*.
Reproduced courtesy of Unilever

WOUNDED SOLDIERS HAVING TEA AT CARROW ABBEY

© From *Carrow Works Magazine*. Reproduced courtesy of Unilever

her work before Christmas 1916 and her friend, Maude Lovick, joined her soon after. They both later qualified to wear the Red Cross uniform.

One significant contribution made at Colman's was the formation of a Carrow Works Contingent of the British Red Cross Society who helped to convey wounded soldiers from Norwich's railway stations to local military hospitals. A photograph of the Colman's men in the *Carrow Works Magazine* suggests that the Carrow Works ambulance was made available for their use.

The Colman family made the tranquil grounds of Crown Point available for those convalescing and also gave direct support. On 19 May 1916, Mrs Stuart entertained a party of soldiers from the Lakenham Military Hospital and the Bracondale Red Cross Hospital at a tea party in the garden at Carrow Abbey. On another occasion Southwell organised a 'treat' at the Norwich Hippodrome to which he invited wounded soldiers, nurses, Red Cross workers, the city constabulary, and others. The *Eastern Daily Press* reported that 'a sufficient number of tramcars had been chartered to bring the party from their different points, and also to convey them back after the performance'. The end of the show prompted a deafening cheer, followed by the 'Jolly Good Fellow' chorus.

CONNECTIONS
WITH THE FRONT

The community at Colman's kept in touch with and supported their families, colleagues and friends at the front through letters and parcels. These connections to home were a vital reassurance for soldiers, undoubtedly providing emotional comfort to those in service.

A great deal of Colman's Mustard was sent to men on the front. Pictures in the *Carrow Works Magazine* depicted tins battered by enemy fire, and mustard was sent to British prisoners in Germany. A letter from Mr D. Hotson Palmer stated that:

> the Germans don't want Colman's Mustard, as they have seen enough of the tins it comes over in. There are thousands of Mustard tins used for hand grenades.

The medicinal properties of mustard were also promoted to soldiers returning from the front lines, with claims that a mustard bath would 'soak out the grime of the trenches'.

PARCELS FROM HOME

Many parcels were sent out to the front by Colman's workers attending the Men's First Day School. These parcels were sent throughout the war and included practical items such as clean shirts and vests, and boric acid ointment for the treatment of wounds. The parcels also contained items to provide comfort and remind soldiers of home, such as copies of local newspapers, *The New Testament* and a motto card.

MUSTARD TIN RELICS FROM THE FRONT

© From *Carrow Works Magazine*. Reproduced courtesy of Unilever

Parcels were also sent overseas. Of those that went further than France, four went to the Dardanelles (Turkey) and one to HMS Ark Royal – somewhere on the sea! These parcels contained:

- 1 box of Lung Tabloids
- 1 pair of socks
- 1 khaki coloured handkerchief
- 1 cake of soap

The "first luxury" of a man on leave is a Mustard Bath—a bath to which has been added a tablespoonful or so of mustard. It soaks *out* the grime of the trenches and soaks *in* the tonic properties of the mustard.

Colman's Mustard Bath

"Let Muster Mustard prepare your bath."

© Illustrated War News Limited

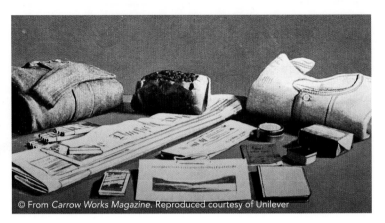

© From *Carrow Works Magazine*. Reproduced courtesy of Unilever

- 6 packets of cigarettes
- Nightlights
- Safety matches in case
- 1 *Norfolk News*
- 1 tin toffee
- 1 pocket testament
- 1 motto card
- 2 booklets
- 1 shirt
- 1 wool helmet
- 1 box Oxo cubes

Surprisingly there were no Colman's products!

This contact from home helped keep the connection with the men of Norwich and Colman's whilst they were at the front. First Day School member Ernest Nichols had written a letter to Mr Beales at Carrow Works, dated just four days before his death. He made a reference to the School in this, his last letter:

> There is not a day goes by that I do not think about the good old Firm ... I think about you a great deal, especially on Sundays ... although not with you in body ... I am with you in mind and thought.

SANDBAGS FOR TRENCHES

Colman's workers found other ways to help soldiers at the front, with members of the Women's First Day School giving up their dinner hours to make sandbags for use in the trenches in France. Specific instructions had to be adhered to:

> They must not be heavy but strong, to stand wet and weight. [...] Mouth of bag to be left open and a piece of stout string two feet long must be tied on, three inches below mouth, ready to close when bag is filled.

The women's efforts were recognised by the mother of a captain in the Royal Field Artillery who wrote:

> I have sent my son 350 sandbags. He is delighted with them, and says his observation post has been safe for the first time since the last shift.

The women also helped in other practical ways by knitting socks and making garments for the men on active service, on behalf of the Lady Mayoress' Needlework Guild. It was important however that

WOMEN'S FIRST DAY SCHOOL MEMBERS MAKING SANDBAGS FOR THE WAR EFFORT

© From *Carrow Works Magazine*. Reproduced courtesy of Unilever

MOTOR AMBULANCE PRESENTED BY MR & MRS COLMAN, CROWN POINT, NORWICH TO THE 9TH BASE HOSPITAL, LE HAVRE, WITH DRIVER PRIVATE LE FEAVER

© From *Carrow Works Magazine*. Reproduced courtesy of Unilever

socks for the troops should be knitted in natural-coloured wool only, as poisoning from a coloured dye could prove troublesome. One grateful recipient sent a letter thanking one of the members of the Women's First Day School – her name had been sown in one of the mitts.

Dear Mrs Roberts
I hope you will excuse me for taking the liberty of writing you these few lines of thanks for the mitts. I was very much in need of them, nothing could be of better use. I must tell you that I am a Transport Driver, and I am a Welshman, and been out here since it all started. Well, I think this is all I can say, so thanks very much.
I remain,
Yours faithfully
No 1020, Driver W Leary
British Expeditionary Force

The Colman family also provided items for the front. Mr and Mrs Colman presented an ambulance to the 9th Base Hospital, Le Havre. The vehicle was built to hold four stretchers, and arranged so that the wounded could be looked after during transit. Medical stores, together with a supply of tea, chocolate and cigarettes, were also sent, along with the driver Private Le Feaver. Another ambulance, given to the Red Cross by Sir Jeremiah Colman, was reported to have transported over 500 wounded men in just one month in 1915.

Sir Jeremiah also gave substantial financial help to Princess Christian's Hospital Train. The train, which had up to fourteen coaches, was designed to carry four hundred patients. Containing operating rooms and a permanent medical staff, Sir Jeremiah commented that 'the arrangements were little short of extraordinary'.

LETTERS HOME: THE REALITY FROM THE FRONT

Contact with the front was not one-sided. Increasingly as the war progressed, *Carrow Works Magazine* became a conduit for news of the men from the front, publishing their letters, which often contained references to Colman's.

From Gunner Donald Key, Cape Town, South Africa, to Mr Beales, dated 17 July 1917:

> the Firm's wares greet me everywhere I go, and I cannot escape the 'ads'. Near me as I sit writing in this ex-Feather Market is a column from which is suspended a show-card, depicting two children on the sea-shore and a familiar legend relating to Colman's Azure Blue, so you see Colman gets everywhere.

From Sergeant P. H. Brunskill, Egypt, to Mr Woodcock, dated 7 November 1917. He enclosed a snapshot of a poster advertising Starch and Blue:

> I am writing this at Alexandria, where we have been for the last three months or so. The interesting part is that the advertisement is worded in five different languages – English, French, Arabic, Italian and Greek, which gives one an idea of the various nationalities that have to be catered for here.

The extracts from the soldiers' letters not only illustrate that this was a World War with correspondence from the United Kingdom, France, Palestine, India, Egypt, Mesopotamia, South Africa and from those at sea, but also emphasised that Colman's was a global product.

Ethel Belson, who for many years had been connected with Carrow Sunday School as both a scholar and a teacher, travelled to work in a hospital in France. Writing home in July 1918, she said:

> My work is very varied: scrubbing, washing bandages, seeing after the laundry, sewing buttons on shirts. I see plenty of suffering and yet the boys are all so bright and cheerful.

Although much correspondence was upbeat, the sad reality of deaths on the front was shown in the pages of *Carrow Works Magazine*. The obituaries of their former colleagues were sadly but proudly recorded in the Roll of Honour section.

In the case of Private Albert Howlett, a Blue maker at Carrow Works who was one of the first to enlist and who died on 27 April 1917 in Palestine, the *Carrow Works Magazine* of July 1917 wrote:

> A Chaplain of the Forces writes of him: I came into contact frequently with your dear son, being the Chaplain attached to the Ambulance from May last till we marched into Palestine in January, and at our Church Parade and Voluntary Services I met him often. He was a good lad and we all deplore his loss ... Thank God he suffered no pain. He was buried this morning on the side of a green hill near Gaza.

PRIVATE ALBERT HOWLETT, WHO DIED IN GAZA IN 1917

© From *Carrow Works Magazine*. Reproduced courtesy of Unilever

AN ADVERT FOR COLMAN'S FROM ALEXANDRIA, IN FIVE LANGUAGES

© From *Carrow Works Magazine*. Reproduced courtesy of Unilever

A COUNTRY
FIT FOR HEROES?

As the war came to a close, Colman's workers returned from the front lines to a changed Britain. But was it 'a country fit for heroes to live in', as promised by post-war Prime Minister Lloyd George?

THE GREAT FLU PANDEMIC OF 1918-1919
Even as fighting continued through 1918, the global population was about to come under attack from an adversary that would cause even more casualties.

Killing almost three times more than the First World War, the Great Flu Pandemic ravaged communities and affected all. Historians estimate that around 50 million people worldwide lost their lives in the pandemic.

Known in the trenches by its French name, 'la grippe', the outbreak hit Great Britain in waves, peaking at the end of the war and affecting every aspect of military and civilian life. The pandemic even permeated popular song, in a children's nursery rhyme: 'I had a little bird, its name was Enza, I opened the window and in-flu-Enza.'

Colman's workers were amongst those affected, both at home and on the front, and many, including Eva Barber, forewoman of the Blue Department, lost their lives. Others included:

Herbert Powell, from the Engineering Department. Powell joined the Royal Field Artillery as a Gunner in November 1914, served in Egypt for three years, and was then sent to France where, on 11 October 1918, he was admitted to a Military Hospital suffering from influenza. He died on 17 October.

George Temple left school aged fifteen to work for Colman's at Bethnal Green, London and when war broke out he joined the Royal Naval Air Service as an Air Mechanic. Following an attack of influenza, he was taken on board Hospital Ship 'Karapara' where his condition declined rapidly and he died on 3 December 1918, aged twenty-one.

HERBERT POWELL, WHO DIED OF INFLUENZA IN 1918

GEORGE TEMPLE, WHO DIED OF INFLUENZA IN 1918, AGED 21

© From *Carrow Works Magazine*. Reproduced courtesy of Unilever

© From *Carrow Works Magazine*. Reproduced courtesy of Unilever

A NEW COLMAN'S?

The scale of the First World War was unprecedented. It resulted in various political, economic and social tensions playing out across the country. Workers demanded better conditions, and women fought for their right to vote. From the horrors of the war sprung a new social and political confidence amongst the working classes that would help define the new Britain forged in the latter half of the twentieth century.

In 1918, Colman's introduced significant changes at the factory in order to reduce the chances of industrial action. The eight-hour day, postponed from 1914, was introduced. Men would work a standard week of forty-eight hours, except the 'trades' whose hours would be agreed with the unions. Women were to work forty-four hours per week.

On 13 August 1918, the directors introduced a Works Council, to promote greater co-operation between employers and employees, and hopefully eliminate industrial strife after the war. Matters could be raised by employees via a sealed letter handed to the appointed Secretary.

Requests included moving the payment of wages to a Friday morning, so that wives could shop in the afternoon, and better hot and cold water systems for the baths for the boiler men and coalmen. Other agreements included the negotiation of wages by trade unions, and that men returning from the war would receive the current wage in their department, irrespective of any additional war pension they were receiving if disabled. The Works Council subsequently ran the Social Scheme, set up an Allotments Committee and a Housing Advisory Committee, and took over the running of other schemes from the directors.

On 6 November 1918, it was announced that all employees who had worked for Colman's for a full year would receive one week's holiday on full pay. This was unprecedented in industry as workers previously only received the obligatory bank holidays.

Following the Armistice, the first meeting of the Social Scheme Central Committee was held on 9 May 1919 when the directors immediately contributed £100 to re-start the Social Scheme. The basis for a range of new classes and clubs was established, and arrangements were agreed for three tennis courts and work at Lakenham Cricket Ground. Renovations to the Club House were already underway following its release by the military, with a view to organising a programme of educational events for forthcoming winter evenings.

Colman's was an exceptional company in many ways. Not only did they excel at business but they were very altruistic in their treatment of employees and the community in which they lived. A philosophy of 'from cradle to grave' epitomised the family's style of nonconformist philanthropy.

THE FIRST WORKS COUNCIL

CONCLUSION

From the firm's outset in 1814, the Colman family pioneered a 'from cradle to grave' ethos to support and care for their employees and families. Within a century, from out of the Carrow Works factory, grew not only the largest workforce in Norfolk, but also a large extended 'family' who lived, worked and played in and around the south of Norwich.

As the company entered its second century of trading, the First World War was having a brutal impact on the factory and the city, fracturing all corners of Europe and the world. But the solid social foundations built by Colman's over that previous peaceful century stood the factory in good stead, providing caring support and much needed financial assistance, both during and after the war. In turn the workers remained loyal, with many men returning to work at Carrow in 1918, to a company which would continue to thrive economically, with its philanthropic ideals stronger than ever before.

The *Colman's Connections* project has in its own way created a Colman's family. We would like to extend a huge thank you to all the wonderful and dedicated Colman's Detectives, the Heritage Heroes and the many partners who have generously offered their facilities, resources and time to make the mammoth task of revealing Colman's story during the First World War thoroughly enjoyable and fascinating.

There is still a flourishing mustard industry in Norwich and many people talk proudly about their relatives who worked at Carrow Works decades ago. Many of the houses built for Colman's employees survive today, and the iconic factory on the banks of the river Wensum can still be seen from the opposing bank. We can only conclude that Norwich will continue to have, for many decades to come, a Colman's connection!